CECIL COUNTY
PUBLIC LIBRARY

DEC 2 4 2014

ark Ave
D 21921

D1074240

Boa Constrictors

BY ELIZABETH RAUM

amicus
high interest

Amicus High Interest is an imprint of Amicus
P.O. Box 1329, Mankato, MN 56002
www.amicuspublishing.us

Copyright © 2014 Amicus. International copyright reserved in
all countries. No part of this book may be reproduced in any
form without written permission from the publisher.

Library of Congress Cataloging-in-Publication Data
Raum, Elizabeth.
 Boa constrictors / by Elizabeth Raum.
     pages cm. -- (Snakes)
 Summary: "Describes boa constrictors including what they
eat, where they live, and information about their life cycle and
interaction with humans"--Provided by publisher.
 Audience: K to Grade 3.
 ISBN 978-1-60753-372-6 (library binding) -- ISBN 978-1-
60753-420-4 (ebook)
1. Boa constrictor--Juvenile literature. I. Title.
 QL666.O63R383 2014
 597.96'7--dc23

                            2012036388

Editor   Wendy Dieker
Series Designer   Kathleen Petelinsek
Page production   Red Line Editorial, Inc.

Photo Credits
Kitti Sukhonthanit/Shutterstock Images, cover; John Pitcher/
iStockphoto, 5; David Whaley/Dreamstime, 6; Pichugin
Dmitry/Shutterstock Images, 9; Patrick K. Campbello/
Shutterstock Images, 10; Mitchell Kranz/Shutterstock Images,
13; Neil Rankins/123RF, 14; Mauro Rodrigues/123RF, 17;
Shutterstock Images, 19; Michael Zysman/Dreamstime,
20; Minden Pictures/SuperStock, 23; Diane White Rosier/
iStockphoto, 24; Rechitan Sorin/Shutterstock Images, 26;
Constance Knox/iStockphoto, 29

Printed in Printed in the United States at Corporate Graphics
in North Mankato, Minnesota
4-2013 / 1149
10 9 8 7 6 5 4 3 2 1

Table of Contents

A Watchful Boa

A large snake rests at the edge of the
rain forest. A small village is nearby.
Farmers work in the fields. Children are
playing. The snake, a boa constrictor,
climbs a tree and curls around a branch.
The boa hasn't eaten for several days.
It is hungry.

An emerald boa coils around a tree branch.

This boa tries to hide in a tree.

 Q Do boas attack people?

The boa stays out of sight. Its coloring helps it hide in the branches. If the children get too close, the boa will slither away. Boas are peaceful snakes. They are big, but they are not poisonous. The children are not in danger. The hungry boa will hunt when night falls. It will find a squirrel or rat to eat.

 No. Even children are too big for boas to eat.

Boa constrictors often live in clearings at the edge of a rain forest. Some live in woodlands, grasslands, or dry desert lands. Their home area, or **habitat**, is in Mexico, Central America, and South America. Boas are **cold-blooded**. This means that their body temperature changes when the outside temperature changes. That's why they live in warm places.

Some boas live in warm desert areas.

About Boas

There are about 50 **species**, or kinds, of boas. The biggest boas grow to between 9 and 15 feet (2.7 and 4.5 m) long. They weigh about 100 pounds (45 kg). That's about as much as a seventh grade boy. Don't worry, though. Boas are big, but most boas are calm.

A rainbow boa can grow up to 6 feet (2 m) long.

Boas like to hide. Their color makes hiding easy. Most are light brown with dark brown markings. The marks are shaped like a saddle. They become red near the boa's tail. Three stripes run along a boa's head. These marks all help boas blend in with the ground and trees.

This boa's marks look a little like tree bark and leaves.

A boa hangs on a tree branch.

 How do boas climb trees?

Boas do not like water. They stay away from lakes and rivers. But you can find them in other places. They like rocks and fields. They even lie on tree branches or hang from tree limbs. Boas are strong climbers.

 Boas use their scales to grip tree limbs. Strong muscles in their backs, sides, and belly push their bodies upward.

Boas move forward in a straight line. First, a boa makes its ribs stiff. Then the scales on the boa's belly lift to push it forward. Finally, the boa straightens out. It lifts again, and pushes ahead. Boas are not fast. They only go about one mile an hour (1.6 km/h).

Boas move slowly along in a straight line.

Time for Dinner

Boas hunt at night. They wait for **prey** to come close. Their jawbones feel movement around them. Snap! They use their sharp teeth to grab the prey. Boas coil their body around the prey and squeeze. The prey cannot breathe. Its heart stops, and it dies. Boas eat rats, squirrels, lizards, and birds. They like bats, too. Bigger boas may eat iguanas or porcupines.

 How do boas catch bats?

A boa uses its sharp teeth to grab a mouse to eat.

 Boas hang from tree branches or at openings of caves. When bats fly by, the boas swat them out of the air. Yum!

Open wide! A boa's jaws can stretch wide to eat prey.

 Q Do boas eat the bones, too?

Boas can tell when their prey is dead. Then they swallow the meal. Their jaws stretch open very wide. The prey goes in headfirst. Gulp! Strong stomach muscles push the prey inside. The boa won't need to eat for another 4 to 6 days.

 Yes. Boa stomach juices are very strong. When a boa eats a porcupine, all it leaves behind is a couple of quills.

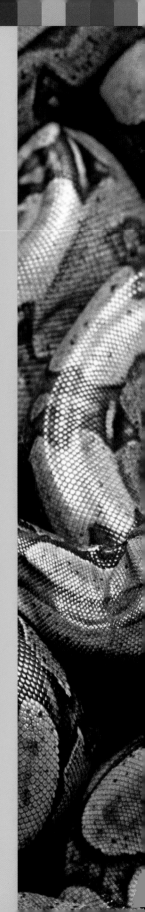

Baby Boas

Boas usually live alone. Male and female boas come together to **mate**. Then they go their separate ways.

Female boas have babies every other year. The babies grow inside their mother's body for 5 to 8 months. Then, they are born live. A female boa has 10 to 64 babies at a time.

Many baby boas wiggle around soon after birth.

Baby boas are only 17 to 20 inches (43 to 50 cm) long at birth. They grow quickly and go off on their own. Boas shed their old skin as they grow. The skin splits near the mouth and peels back. It takes several days to shed their skin. The new skin is smooth and beautiful.

As a boa grows, it leaves its skin behind.

A jaguar prowls for a meal.
It might find a young boa.

Watch Out, Little Boa!

Young boas must watch out for enemies. Jaguars, large lizards, and other **mammals** kill and eat them. Older boas can defend themselves more easily. They bite their enemies. Boa teeth are sharp. But boas do not have **fangs** with poison. A boa's bite won't kill you, but it hurts!

Many zoos and museums have boas that you can visit and enjoy. Boas are popular pets. But caring for a boa is not easy. They are big, live a long time, and require special food. They eat live mice, rats, and bats. Boas must be handled carefully because they are strong. Boas are large, powerful snakes.

 How long do boas live?

Even in the zoo, boas like
to coil around branches.

 Most boas live about 20 years.

Glossary

cold-blooded To have the same temperature as the outside air or environment.

fang A long, sharp tooth filled with poison.

habitat Home; the place where an animal is usually found.

mammal An animal that gives birth to live young and has hair on its body.

mate To come together to create children.

prey An animal that is hunted for food.

rain forest A tropical forest with tall evergreen trees in an area of heavy rainfall.

species A kind or type of animal.

Read More

Jones, Cede. *Boa Constrictor*. Killer Snakes. New York: Gareth Stevens, 2011.

Nichols, Catherine. *Emerald Boas: Rain Forest Undercover*. Disappearing Acts. New York: Bearport, 2010.

Sexton, Colleen A. *Boa Constrictors*. Snakes Alive! Minneapolis, Minn: Bellwether Media, 2010.

Websites

Boa Constrictor Fact Sheet – National Zoo
http://nationalzoo.si.edu/Animals/ReptilesAmphibians/Facts/FactSheets/Boaconstrictor.cfm

Boa Constrictor Facts and Pictures – National Geographic Kids
http://kids.nationalgeographic.com/kids/animals/creaturefeature/boa/

San Diego Zoo's Animal Bytes: Boas
http://www.sandiegozoo.org/animalbytes/t-boa.html

Index

About the Author

Elizabeth Raum has worked as a teacher, librarian, and writer. She has written dozens of books for young readers. She really enjoyed learning more about snakes. "Snakes are amazing," she says. "But I wouldn't want one for a pet." Visit her website at http://elizabethraum.net.